Reduce, Reuse, Recycle

Energy

Alexandra Fix

Heinemann Library
Chicago, Illinois

© **2008 Heinemann Library**
a division of Reed Elsevier Inc.
Chicago, Illinois

Customer Service 888-454-2279
Visit our website at www.heinemannraintree.com

Designed by Steven Mead and Debbie Oatley
Printed in China by South China Printing Company Limited

12 11 10 09 08
10 9 8 7 6 5 4 3 2 1

10-digit ISBNs: 1-4034-9715-X (hc) 1-4034-9723-0 (pb)

Library of Congress Cataloging-in-Publication Data
Fix, Alexandra, 1950-
  Energy / Alexandra Fix.
    p. cm. -- (Reduce, reuse, recycle)
  Includes bibliographical references and index.
  ISBN 978-1-4034-9715-4 (hc) -- ISBN 978-1-4034-9723-9 (pb)
  1. Energy conservation--Juvenile literature. 2. Power resources--Juvenile literature. 3. Recycling (Waste, etc.)--Juvenile literature. I. Title.
  TJ163.23.F59 2007
  333.791'6--dc22
                        2007002783

Acknowledgments
The author and publisher are grateful to the following for permission to reproduce copyright material: Alamy pp. **20** (Chris Fredricksson), **21** (Mark Boulton); Ardea pp. **9** (Arthur Hayward), **15** (Francois Gohier), **25** (Jack A. Bailey); Corbis pp. **4** (Ashley Cooper), **5** (Royalty Free), **6** (Royalty Free), **7** (Royalty Free), **12** (Alberto Esteves/EPA), **18** (Steve Chenn), **22** (SIE Productions/Zefa), **23** (Tim Street-Porter/Beateworks), **24** (Paul Thompson), **26** (Royalty Free), **27** (TH-Foto/Zefa); Naturepl.com pp. **8** (Aflo), **13** (Aflo), **16** (Pete Cairns), **19** (Dave Noton); Photolibrary.com pp. **10** (Dynamic Graphics Ltd.), **11** (Index Stock Imagery), **17** (Botanica), **28** (Fernando Bengoechea); Reuters p. **14** (Stefano Paltera/Handout XX).

Cover photograph reproduced with permission of Alamy/oote boe.

Every effort has been made to contact copyright holders of any material reproduced in this book. Any omissions will be rectified in subsequent printings if notice is given to the publisher.

Disclaimer
All Internet addresses (URLs) given in this book were valid at the time of going to press. However, due to the dynamic nature of the Internet, some addresses may have changed or ceased to exist since publication. While the author and the publishers regret any inconvenience this may cause readers, no responsibility for any such changes can be accepted by either the author or the publishers.

Contents

Some words are shown in bold, **like this**. You can find out what they mean by looking in the glossary.

What Is Energy Waste?

We use energy to make things work. Nearly everything around us uses energy. Most of the energy we use comes from burning coal, oil, and natural gas.

Coal, oil, and natural gas are called **fossil fuels**.

Oil is pumped from the ground with machines like this one.

When we use more energy than we need, we waste energy. People are using up the Earth's supply of coal, oil, and natural gas. Once these sources of energy are gone, they cannot be replaced.

How Do We Use Energy?

Natural gas is a form of energy we use to cook meals and heat and cool our homes. Oil is a form of energy we use to make big machines work, such as cars, boats, and airplanes.

↑ Our bodies make energy from the foods we eat.

Many kitchen items need electricity to work. ↑

Electricity is a form of energy that makes many items work. Anything that plugs into the wall uses electricity. Lamps, computers, refrigerators, televisions, and toaster ovens all use electricity.

Where Does Energy Come From?

There are many sources of energy. These include the sun, wind, and ocean waves. We can use these sources of energy to make **electricity**.

Most of the energy on Earth comes from the sun.

Dinosaur remains from long ago turned into fuel we use today.

We can also make electricity by burning coal, oil, and natural gas. These materials are called **fossil fuels**. They are the remains of animals and plants that died millions of years ago.

Nuclear power plants can create energy to make electricity for homes, schools, and offices.

Many places use **nuclear energy** to make **electricity**. Nuclear energy comes from the energy stored inside a certain type of **atom**. Atoms are tiny, invisible particles that make up everything around us.

We can also make electricity with **geothermal energy**. This form of energy comes from hot liquid rock trapped deep inside the Earth.

People can make electricity and heat buildings by pumping up heated water from deep underground.

What Are Nonrenewable Energy Sources?

Coal, oil, and natural gas are our main energy sources. These materials are **nonrenewable resources**. Once we use them up, they will be gone forever.

Oil is a nonrenewable resource that we use to make cars run. ⟶

People are starting to use corn as an energy source. Corn can be grown and does not pollute the air.

Nonrenewable resources **pollute** the air when they are burned for energy. Some scientists believe that air **pollution** is causing the Earth's **climate** to change. This is called **global warming**.

What Are Renewable Energy Sources?

Some of the energy we use comes from **renewable resources**. These are resources we will never run out of. Most renewable energy sources do not cause air **pollution**.

Solar cars run on electricity made by the sun.

A field of windmills can make electricity from wind power. ↑

Sunshine and wind are renewable energy sources. Both of these sources can be used to make **electricity**.

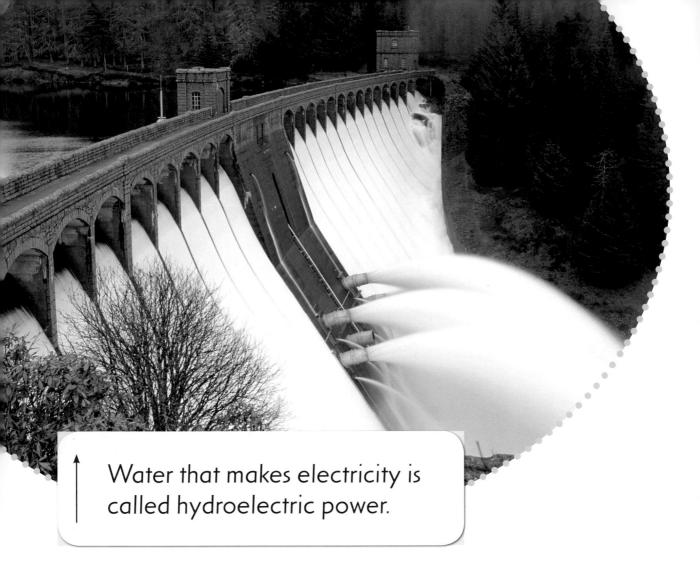

Water that makes electricity is called hydroelectric power.

Water is a **renewable resource** that we can use for energy. Dams and waterfalls can be used to make **electricity**. Scientists are also learning how to use water waves to make electricity.

Trees and plants are renewable energy sources. We can grow more trees and plants as we use them. They can be burned to create energy.

Burning wood is the oldest use of **bioenergy**.

What Happens When We Waste Energy?

When we waste energy, we waste **nonrenewable resources** such as coal, oil, and natural gas. Once we use up these resources, they will be gone forever.

We can save energy by turning down the heat in our homes.

Factory smoke gives off harmful gases.

When coal, oil, and natural gas are burned, they create air **pollution**. Some scientists believe that this is causing **global warming**. By using less energy, we can help reduce air pollution.

How Can We Use Less Energy?

There are many ways to use less energy at home. You can use less hot water to save energy. Try washing things less often. Towels and most clothing can be used more than once.

Dry clothes outside on sunny days.

Fluorescent lightbulbs last longer than regular lightbulbs.

Lights use energy. When you leave a room, turn off the lights. You can also ask family members to buy fluorescent lightbulbs. They use less energy than regular lightbulbs.

21

Turn off and unplug appliances as soon as you are finished with them.

Many household items use energy even when they are not being used. Unplug **appliances** such as televisions, toaster ovens, and stereos when you are not using them.

Use appliances that take less energy to work. You can use a fan instead of air conditioning when it is hot outside. Walk or ride a bike whenever you can instead of riding in a car. Cars use oil, a **nonrenewable resource**.

Trees planted near houses can help keep them cool.

How Can Recycling Save Energy?

We can save energy by **recycling** products that are made out of glass, plastic, metal, and paper. It takes less energy to make items from recycled materials than it does to make new items.

Some communities have separate garbage cans for materials that can be recycled.

When items are not recycled, they are buried in a landfill.

Separate recycling materials when you use them at home or at school. You can then bring them to a recycling center. Then they are taken to a factory, where they are broken down and used to make a new item.

How Can You Take Action?

Ask family and friends to be more careful about using **electricity**. Remind others to turn off lights when they leave a room to save energy.

Turning off lights is one easy way to save energy.

It takes less energy to recycle plastic, glass, metal, and paper than to make them new.

Find out where your local **recycling** center is located. At home and at school, you can ask about recycling. By reducing energy waste, we can help keep our planet clean.

Be An Energy Detective!

Ask an adult to help you with this project.

Complete the following steps to learn more about how much energy is used in your home.

1. Get a notebook and pencil.
2. Look around each room in your house.
3. Write down everything that uses gas. Record what you find for each room.

4. Write down everything that uses **electricity**. Record what you find for each room.

Think of ways your family can reduce the amount of energy you use. Were all the electrical items plugged in? Items that are plugged in use energy even when they are not turned on.

Fast Facts

The United States uses one-fourth of the world's energy sources.

Most Americans use 500 gallons of gasoline every year.

Every American throws away around 1,000 pounds of garbage in one year.

Glossary

appliance   household machine, such as a dishwasher or toaster, that usually runs on electricity or gas

atom   one of the tiny particles that makes up all things

bioenergy   living things that can be burned to create energy

climate   typical weather of a place over a period of time

electricity   form of energy that can be used to create light, heat, and power

fossil fuel   remains of animals and plants that died millions of years ago and slowly turned into coal, oil, and natural gas

geothermal energy   water heated by hot, liquid rock trapped deep inside the earth

global warming   change in the Earth's climate

nonrenewable resource material of the Earth that cannot be replaced by nature

nuclear energy   form of energy that comes from using atoms

pollute   harm the air, soil, or water with chemicals or wastes

pollution   wastes and poisons in the air, water, or soil

recycling   breaking down and using again

renewable resource   material that can be replaced by nature

30

Find Out More

Books to Read

Oxlade, Chris. *How We Use Coal*. Chicago: Raintree, 2004.

Oxlade, Chris. *How We Use Oil*. Chicago: Raintree, 2004.

Manolis, Kay. *Energy*. Racine, WI: Bellwether Media, 2007.

Web Sites

The Environmental Protection Agency works to protect the air, water, and land. www.epa.gov/kids.

Earth911 is an organization that gives information about where you can recycle in your community. www.earth911.org/master.asp?s=kids&a=kids/kids.asp.

The Energy Information Administration has a student Web page: www.eia.doe.gov/kids/energyfacts/index.html.

Index